Giving

Non-Governmental Organizations (NGOs) a Competitive Edge

By

Larry Roeder, MS

Former UN Affairs Director, WSPA

October 16, 2018

Giving NGO's an Edge.

Giving NGO's an Edge.

Mr. Roeder a former Policy Adviser on Disaster Management at the U.S. Department of State, as well as Director of United Nations Affairs at WSPA, a British non-profit. In addition, he teaches methods of diplomacy. Currently, Mr. Roeder is President of a non-profit that advocates for a culturally diversified society.

Contents

Introduction

This handbook introduces guidelines of behavior that will place an NGO (non-governmental organization) a competitive edge ahead of others for donations and political influence.

Emphasis is placed on how to entice government officials to support NGO policies and legislative priorities. Known as "Protocol" in diplomatic circles, this is a very large, complex topic that blends cultural sensitivity with practical procedures. However, the basic concept is simple. At meetings, parties, conferences and other events, the NGO representative is considered the symbolic representative of his or her organization in the same way an Ambassador is for a country. To an extent, the NGO representative should also be a considered a symbol of all NGOs. Thus, what this person does or says could influence how all NGOs are treated by governments in an emergency.

A representative is never thought to acting alone, but instead on behalf of his NGO or coalition. Keep in mind as well that although these "protocol rules" can seem artificial at times, understanding them will impress donors and policy makers. That's the goal of this handbook, to convince officialdom to go in a specific direction.

Many complain that protocol is really about how to wear a white tie or where to put the seats at a formal dinner, perhaps about not wearing brown shoes after six or pearls in the morning, or not looking at a watch during a party, to avoid appearing bored (Boritz,

Email Discussion on Diplomatic Practice, 2010). That's incorrect. The rules of behavior we propose are really about the art of using an understanding about politeness and local customs to achieve an operational goal. A good example is found in the fabled representative of Peace-Action in New York, Ms. Judy Lerner, who often hosts small cocktail parties in one of her homes. She has a simple graciousness and ability to create an atmosphere where people of differing opinions can pleasantly debate and come to agreement.

To provide real-world authenticity, officers in the Secretariat of the U.S. Department of State made suggestions for this book, as well as the Office of International conferences and the Office of Protocol. The Protocol and Liaison Service of the United Nations was also very helpful, as were the works of Mary Jane McCaffree, a protocol specialist at the Department of State whose book has been a bible for diplomats for over 30 years (McCaffree & Innis, 1977). There was also a book by Ambassador Mary Mel French (French, 2010). Finally, Joanna Morrini, Ceremonial Office, Protocol Directorate, Foreign and Commonwealth Office, as well as Moritt Boritz, a curator in the Danish National Museum were both very helpful. There is also <u>Protocol for the Modern Diplomat</u> by the Foreign Service Institute. Also, nearly every country has its own manual, some of which I studied for this book. If a non-profit intends to work in a foreign land, it should also study that country's handbook.

One of the most overused statements about "protocol" is that the term comes from the Greek phrase meaning "the first glue." As McCaffree pointed out, rules of protocol go back as far as Cyrus the Great in Persepolis, over 2,500 years ago; throughout history, even though the rules have changed, the intent has been the same, to help make and keep useful connections, which is how an NGO official should see effort. Effective networking in this manner will enable an NGO to influence legislation, achieve monetary grants or permission to enter a war zone when others are deterred.

In past times, Ambassadors were important because they came from important governments; however now the system is largely a meritocracy. The Ambassador of even the smallest, least powerful nation like the Seychelles can influence major events just as ably as a French Ambassador if he or she has great protocol skills. Thus, this is one of the most important tools for an NGO of any size when communicating with a diplomat, a rebel in the field, a donor or local political leader.

Communication between governments or the UN with NGOs is often strained because many NGOs are considered to be informal, biased, and uninformed in protocol – even if they have a lot of substantive knowledge. Some are often called extreme. To overcome that barrier, every member of the team must comport himself as a diplomat, which Boritz once said meant someone whose personal characteristics are truthfulness, calmness, accuracy, patience, good humor, modesty and loyalty. More precise and workable skills like self-control, an ability to formulate one's thoughts, an ability to read a situation, an instinct for discreet flattery and a talent for contacting people are also important. (Boritz, The Hidden Culture of Diplomatic Practice, 1998).

2 Attending Social Events

In the small-community environment of the United Nations, HQ cities like New York, Rome, Geneva, Bangkok and Nairobi in particular, NGO representatives will have frequent opportunities to meet Ambassadors in social events and major conferences. My recommendation is that representatives should not be shy about reaching out to foreign diplomats of any rank, shake their hands and make introductions. While the representatives should explain his or her agency's mission, keep remarks simple and short, focusing on how the NGO's mission or objective relates or enhances the diplomat's own mandate. That simple act, especially if done regularly, will enable an NGO representative to be invited to have additional meetings with policy makers on priority topics. The Ambassador might also come to an NGO event.

The diplomatic community in many countries is small and often welcoming to NGO representatives, therefore. NGOs need to make a point of attending national holidays celebrations at embassies and other diplomatic missions, "become a regular part of the scene." That way, the NGO will learn who best to deal with on issues and Ambassadors and agency chiefs will be more apt to return calls.

3 Accreditation, Badges and Business Cards

Before trying to go to a meeting at an international organization, the representative probably must be accredited in his or her own right or work for an accredited NGO. Every conference or meeting has its own attendance rules. Learn them well in advance. In

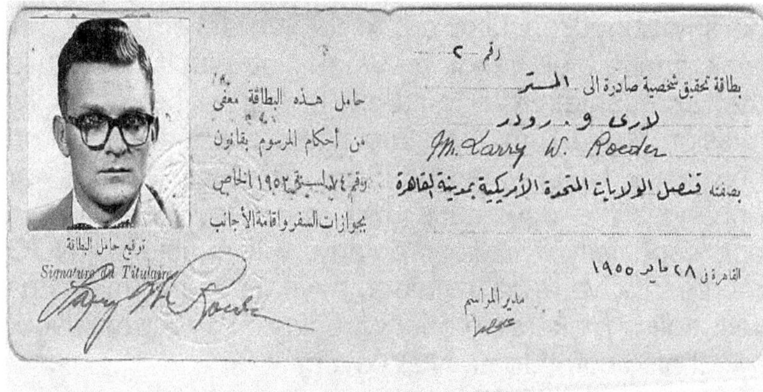

Figure 1 Personal Collection of Larry Roeder

addition, some conferences will limit the size of a delegation. On the other hand, though attending an event might require some form of accreditation, many NGOs and UN agencies also foster discussion groups on the Internet, which require no accreditation.

Assuming accreditation is needed, which office does it? A common misunderstanding is that the United Nations as a whole accredits NGOs. Not so; the UN is a conglomeration of institutions: organs, conferences, organizations, departments, and agencies, each with its own badge system. In each case, to be accredited, the Secretariat should be consulted. The delegation needs to quickly figure out which UN entity it will visit and then decide if it must be accredited in more than one city; some agencies have both New York and Geneva offices. If an NGO is accredited to either ECOSOC (Economic and Social Council) or DPI (Department of Public Information), the badge will allow access to most UN facilities in NY, though special arrangements may be required at UNHCR (UN High Commissioner for Refugees).

National agencies around the world and at the Geneva, Bangkok and Nairobi UN compounds all have their own badge systems. DPI and ECOSOC badges can also be helpful for entering the UN compound in Nairobi and elsewhere, but prior authorization is required. Nairobi is home for the UN Environmental Organization (UNEP), and most relief operations in the Horn of Africa. In Rome, the World Food Program (WFP) and the Food and Agriculture Organization (FAO), both organizations anyone interested in food security should get to know. Each requires separate ground passes. Paris is home to UNESCO, which is responsible for protecting culture, education and science, as well as the Organization of Economic Cooperation and Development (OECD), and the World Health Organization for Animals (OIE), the last two of which are not under the UN. A separate ground pass will be needed for each.

If an NGO gains accreditation to ECOSOC, the badge will allow its representatives access to compounds in Geneva and New York and many of the UN agencies in both cities. Access is also possible for the regional economic commissions. Authority to do this is granted by Article 71 of the UN Charter. UN DPI: The relationship with the UN Department of Public Information (DPI) with NGOs is almost as old as that of ECOSOC. In 1946, The General Assembly, in its resolution 13 (I), instructed DPI and its branch offices to: ". . actively assist and encourage national information services, educational institutions and other governmental and nongovernmental organizations of all kinds interested in spreading information about the United Nations. For this and other purposes, it should operate a fully equipped reference service, brief or supply lecturers, and make available its publications, documentary films, film strips, posters and other exhibits for use by these agencies and organizations." In 1968, the Economic and Social Council, by Resolution 1297 (XLIV) of 27 May, called on DPI to associate NGOs, bearing in mind the letter and spirit of its Resolution 1296 (XLIV) of 23 May 1968, which stated that an NGO ". . . shall undertake to support the work of the United Nations and to promote knowledge of its principles and activities, in accordance with its own aims and purposes and the nature and scope of its competence and activities."

NGOs should try for ECOSOC and/or DPI accreditation, keeping in mind that not all UN agencies accept their badges, but be prepared for delays, as much as 2 years for ECOSOC and six months for DPI. For ECOSOC, there are limits on how many passes can be granted for a full year of access. If a staff member will only visit once a year, it is probably better to use "day passes." "Each NGO in consultative status with ECOSOC can designate representatives to obtain passes for the UN premises, valid until 31 December of each year. A maximum of five such passes can be issued for New York, 5 for Geneva, and 5 for Vienna, in addition to the Chief Administrative Officer (CAO) and the President or Chief Executive (2 additional passes)."

Don't abuse badges. Many NGOs try to use their DPI or ECOSOC pass to gain entry to emergency and disaster compounds in Haiti, Africa, and elsewhere. While this might work from time to time, it is illegal, and the authorizing authority might remove the badge. On the other hand, the DPI or ECOSOC pass can authenticate bona fides, making it easier to obtain a local pass.

Whether meeting people in official meetings or social events, an NGO representative should have a bright, understandable business card. When abroad for a major event or an extended time, the back of the card should be in the language of the visited country. When stationed in Bangkok to assist during in the aftermath of a cyclone, my card was in English and Thai, and when posted in France and Egypt was in French and Arabic, etc. The card's contents should include name, position, the NGOs name, and contact information. Business cards usually do not include honorifics, i.e., Mr., Mrs., Ms., or Dr., except for military ranks. (MD or PhD would follow the name when appropriate). Society association letters are not needed in the United States, but this practice may vary in other countries and the British Commonwealth.

- **Administrative Support:** Various organizations facilitate the distribution of literature for NGOs that can't attend meetings, and ECOSOC/NGO and DPI provide ground passes and other administrative support to visiting NGOS. That said, my own opinion is that more help is needed to arrange for inexpensive housing for financially stressed NGOs and the facilitation of visas. Perhaps, working together, the NGO associations along with ECOSOC/NGO and DPI could develop a UN-system wide accrediting system, so that if an NGO is accredited to one agency, it is accredited to all.   Badges issued by DPI and ECOSOC are very helpful; not universal across the various UN HQ sites.

> **Note:**   In New York, a grounds pass should get the holder into ALL UN buildings whether there is a gate like (DC1 and 2), the FF building on 45th Street, or 866 UN Plaza where there are many diplomatic missions. A New York grounds pass won't work in Paris at UNESCO. The NGO will need a local pass for the rue Miolis building and the main building.   The New York pass will generally work in Geneva at the main gate, but other gates will stop NGOs. Saturday access in Geneva is provided by Pass Chalais -- where participants register for special conferences -- for that, Security will have a copy of color-coded special passes, so the officers know if you are NGO, diplomat, etc., these are needed for Saturday access. Rome, Bangkok, Nairobi and other compounds have their own rules. Before heading out, it is best to examine those rules first. (Jordan, 2012)

4 Politeness, Trust, and Respect

Friends are not hard to make in the UN, in governments, or in multilateral bodies. Indeed, as trust is built, officials will help in immeasurable ways, but remember that a contact's first loyalty is to his or her agency. Everything said, even in confidence, will be repeated. This does not mean that lies are appropriate, however. If you cannot promise something, do not. If you do promise something, complete the task. As an example, General George Marshal, usually considered the architect of the war in Europe during World War II, had to build trust with allies and potential adversaries, e.g. Joseph Stalin who said he would trust his life to Marshal. Even if a delegate strongly disagrees with the policies of the official with whom he is working, if trust exists, listening will happen (Abshire, 2005).[1]

Conferences offer many opportunities for NGO delegations to speak in front of Ministers and Ambassadors, and conference workshops are handy for fleshing out concepts and building working level contacts. **Keep it crisp**. Too often, speakers read every word of a PowerPoint presentation, or send an overlong report to HQ that does not truly capture the essence of what happened. If a delegation wants to influence, not just participate, it must translate complex concepts into short clear, practical explanations and recommendations.

Keep in mind that non-native speakers of the NGO delegation's language might fail to fully grasp what the NGO intends. Keep the vocabulary straightforward and speak slowly. A native speaker may think that he or she can choose the right word in a second, but politeness also dictates that he or she gives the others time to work it out. However, keep in mind that there are often shades of meaning behind words that can be lost in translation. If uncertain about the direction of

---

[1] One approach around the problem of repeating confidential information is to resort to Chatham House Rules; but keep in mind that officials often "do repeat."

discussions, feel free to ask questions.

A Delegate should not jump in with the right word very often. Instead, let others develop their own ideas and particular choice of phrase. This is because listening patiently conveys the impression that the listener actually cares about the opinion of others, thereby giving interventions weight. Otherwise, an impatient NGO diplomat will appear to be dominating the discussion. Also, sometimes an NGO delegate's best approach is to use like-minded NGOs or diplomats from UN member states to make the same point. Additionally, some delegations love being the one which finds the right compromise phrase or word; but they are making a mistake. Success isn't about who receives credit. It is about moving an initiative forward. Finally, if the discussions have been in one official language, it isn't unusual for a Delegate to require seeing the official translation in another official language before agreement.

One of the hardest things to teach a negotiator is to speak little and listen a lot. Whether at UN HQ or in the field, the person with whom a delegation is meeting is probably anxious to tell his or her story first, so let him or her. That shows sensitivity and provides a tactical advantage, since every time a delegate speaks, something is revealed about that person's knowledge and thinking process. Let the other side reveal themselves first. Listening also reduces tensions, by the way.

Understanding and Empathy:

Leaving prejudices behind is important. With certain exceptions and within reason, if a rebel promises something[2], his or her word will usually be kept, since the official may want to come back for something else later on. If an NGO team brings trucks of feed for cattle, it may be able to arrange for trucks of food for people. On the other hand, a delegate should not make the mistake of "understanding where the other is coming from." The rebels will certainly be insulted. Listening is empathic. Let the other person explain themselves.

NGO diplomats will find that while negotiations are usually very civil, especially when money, lives or rights are involved, negotiators can be testy. As an example, during the Paris Peace Talks ending WWI, Premier William Hughes of Australia said if a shepherd had to mortgage his home because of the loss of income due to the war, and then lost his home due to foreclosure, then Germany owed him reimbursement. The United States was opposed, so Hughes shouted, saying "Some people in this war have not been so near the fire as we British have, and therefore, being unburned, have a cold, detached view of the situation" (Lamont, 1921). The Americans smiled back.

Smiling is important. A delegate need not worry about knowing everyone but smiling to strangers keeps one alert and reduces tensions. It is also tougher for others to be confrontational if a delegate is considerate, even with staff members that do not perform up to expectations.

Never berate a hapless hotel clerk or waiter who makes a mistake or throw a fit at a meeting. Also, while a

---

[2] Use discretion of course.

diplomat will often have to take hard positions, strongly disagreeing with someone else's position; if a delegate smiles, other delegates tend to smile back, and treat his or her point of view with deference. Never criticize someone in front of another diplomat unless it is accepted that the one being criticized will hear about it.

Thank You:

Rituals surround thank you's. Always thank hosts the following day in writing or by phone. Email "thank you's" do not replace written ones, even in the internet age. They are also signed without courtesy titles (i.e., Carlo Ponti, not Mr. Ponti). Local custom might allow gifts in certain circumstances, but it is better to stick to a hand-written note because they are actually read and in some cases can reap major rewards. The President of the United States once invited me and other members of a task force in which I served to a reception honoring an Ambassador. The reason was that we had supported the Ambassador during a dangerous mission in Lebanon. I sent a hand-written note the following day to the President and First Lady thanking them for inviting the office into their home. A week later the President called me to chat. Turns out the letter was only one of a few.

<u>Tips:</u>

- Parents may be reluctant to leave children or pets behind when attending social functions; however, neither may attend unless invited, with some exception. Otherwise, never assume either is welcome.
- Avoid looking bored, do not look at a watch or smart phone.
- A guest being toasted should remain seated and does not drink to the toast. However, the guest does make a reply and offer a toast to the host.
- Leave a party at a reasonable hour (varies with each country). Leaving early is better than overstaying; briefly thank the host before departure. Custom also dictates that delegation members do not depart prior to the Chief of Delegation. This isn't just fluff, the Chief in a national delegation represents a nation's sovereignty or of an NGO delegation, the "flag" of an NGO or NGO alliance. The practical reason is that issues needing resolution happen at social events, and a Chief needs to be able to make assignments. What if the Chief learns at the event that the following morning another delegation will put forth a surprise motion? The Chief needs to be able to assign one or more members of the team roles ASAP, not after he goes back to the hotel.
- There are cultural differences about casual conversation, so it is best to learn in advance what is appropriate. Definitely do not feel compelled to offer personal information. Even when working in a culture where these questions are permitted, do not ask them.

Discussing children or food is rude in some cultures, not others.
- Even color can be a problem. In Liberia, dead people are taken away in white bags, not black, an essential fact discovered by relief workers fighting the Ebola outbreak in 2014.
- When mingling, keep casual conversations brief and mingle and meet as many people as possible.
- In some countries, an invitation for 8:00 p.m. means arriving precisely at 8:00 p.m. In other countries, it means no earlier than 9:30 p.m. To avoid awkward and embarrassing situations, ask questions in advance.

5 Gifts:

Be careful of gifts and gift-giving. NGOs often leave medallions and certificates, which is fine. They are low cost advertisements. Also fine is giving flowers to a helpful delegation but receiving or presenting large gifts is generally a bad idea. However, if gifts cannot be refused, they should be accepted in the name of the entire NGO, not for oneself. Former Secretary General Kofi Annan showed how to do this when a rebel leader I also worked with in South Sudan, offered Kofi some cattle. Understanding that to refuse the cattle would have insulted the rebel, Annan said "I accept these cattle and would urge your leaders to keep them for me until that proper time when I would ask that they be slaughtered to feed the widows and children who have suffered so much through this conflict." Like Annan, find a clever solution that fits the culture. (UN, 2005).

One of the most common gifts is to offer coffee or a meal (of modest cost). Though an opportunity to quietly reflect on an issue, NGO representatives need to be aware that some governments place limits on the value of the meal being offered, lest it appear to be a bribe. The carefully selected bottle of wine or bunch of flowers can be an effective tool when invited to someone's home or in recognition of someone's efforts, but the cost should be modest and proportional to the deed. If wine is the gift, first make sure the recipient actually drinks alcohol. Even if you work for a wealthy NGO, expensive gifts send the wrong signal about NGO priorities.

Expensive gifts can also work in both directions. While on mission to Albania to develop a fresh national economic development plan, I stayed at a tourist hotel. Food was very limited, potatoes, onions, a few tomatoes and cucumbers, only thin meat and kebob, no fish, chicken or many vegetables. Soup was consistently rice and mystery meat. Because the hotel room was quite Spartan, I was offered an apartment in the residence of the Prime Minister, along with great food. Though the access would have been advantageous and the food a welcome change, I refused, due to the gift's magnitude, and to avoid a conflict of interest.

As an example of what one might do, provide flowers to staff officers in the UN and diplomatic missions who go out of their way to be helpful. In one case, I had been trying to attract the attention of an African Ambassador for two weeks with no success. I knew she was very busy, but it was essential that her mission host a meeting of delegations. Finally, I sent her flowers. She called that evening to apologize for not returning emails, engaged in a long conversation about the initiative, and agreed to host the meeting. $30 of flowers delivered personally to the office worked, but if he had spent $100, this would have been excessive. Another common gift is a large memorial coin from the NGO to be placed in an Ambassador's office, something to advertise the NGO. The Ambassador will feel honored and every time the coin is seen, it turns into a free statement of support; but stay away from free pens. They are considered tacky.

Many rituals and customs often surround gift meanings. The type, color, and number of flowers, for example, may have a hidden meaning. In Italy and China, mums are funeral flowers; think twice about bringing them to a dinner party. But in Japan, placing a single petal at the bottom of a wine glass brings long life. A guest may be expected to bring a small gift, or it may be better to bring nothing at all. Once again, ask colleagues and coworkers about local customs.

6 Managing Perceptions

When an NGO Delegate interacts with an Ambassador, the delegate isn't just showing the face of his or her NGO, that Delegate is putting a face on all NGOs. When I grew up in the Foreign Service, every member of the family felt that any public action reflected on the entire Embassy, and America in general.   Penny Laingen, spouse of Bruce **Laingen, Charge d'Affaires** at the US Embassy during the hostage crisis in Tehran, spoke on exactly these points in interviews.

> "The hostage crisis was a terribly public, international crisis, and when I was on television, I think I was, in the minds of the American people, the wife of the Charge d'affairs being held in Tehran. And how I behaved reflected…perhaps on the whole Foreign Service and other Americans abroad" (Fenzi & Nelson, 1994, p. 217).

Laingen's point of view should be in the consciousness of any NGO delegate because NGOs bring a great vigor, intelligence and imagination to diplomatic affairs, and they have been participating in the activities of international organizations for over a century. Refugees depend on NGOs and many issues like land mine destruction would not have happened without NGOs. The agricultural NGOs have also become an important part of the food security and livelihood protection network.

As an example of good work in modern transitional societies, consider the efforts of NGOs in the societies of the former Soviet Union, especially in nations like

Turkmenistan, Uzbekistan, Kazakhstan, Kyrgyzstan and Tajikistan. On the negative side, there is a growing disparity in those countries between the rich and the poor. Corruption is rampant and there is ethnic hatred, such as between the Kyrgyz and Uzbeks; counterbalancing the negative side of these transitional societies, local and international NGOs have been providing many useful services, some never seen before, like Public Diplomacy. Farmer and water usage associations and the like are emerging; and much of the work of these NGOs is done with the United Nations, the World Bank, and the International Red Cross and Red Crescent Movement and with donors like the ECHO and USAID. Every time an NGO official advances this good work, he or she builds up the reputation of all NGOs.

So much has been accomplished by NGOs; yet the record of accomplishment has been uneven, which is why not every government or IO takes NGOs seriously. While the vast majority of NGOs operate as professionally as any world class government delegation, some overstate their success, not recognizing that initiatives that succeed in the UN, for example, are a result of government action, as much as civil society. UN officials detest boasting, especially about false accomplishments, which is the General Assembly of the United Nations laughed at President Trump in 2018. Some forget about team work and see only the NGO world as the font of solutions. Indeed, one need look no further than CITES and the Land Mine Treaty to understand the importance and intellectual weight NGOs can bring. In the end, the world rises and falls together.

7. Receptions and Personal Entertaining

25

Professional government diplomats make entertainment a regular practice at conferences, as part of the "business of business," which should also be the style for NGO diplomats. Inviting local diplomats and government and UN officials widens one's circle of friends among officials and private citizens who might advance an NGO's agenda or even identify donors. It also facilitates the informal exchange of information, affording others an opportunity to hear alternative views. Of course, when planning the event, carefully consider whom to invite and how formal or informal to make the affair, as well as local customs. Invite higher-ranking officials. Their schedules will be tight, but they still might consider a change of pace. Events need not be large, elaborate, or expensive. In many situations, a simple lunch or a backyard barbeque at a home is more effective and enjoyable than an elaborate dinner or reception. Before considering holding a significant social event like a reception at a conference, question whether it will significantly influence voting, or in the case of a bilateral meeting, will it build support with the host government? If the expense is not likely to build such support, consider joining receptions belonging to other organizations. They can be just as effective for networking.

Cautions

While holding a function can look appetizing to supporters, in these times of financial stress, if the event is not going to change votes, it may be more prudent to use those funds elsewhere. Some NGOs want to consider receptions because they give an appearance to the donors that the NGO is successful or powerful. While photos at a diplomatic function can produce the appearance of a vibrant, effective NGO, such pictures are not more effective than well-written reports to the donors on progress. There is a risk that such events will become propaganda, not cost-effective tools.

Consider the Following at Personal Events

- Is the proposed date appropriate? Any conflicts?
- What is social time in the host country? Will guests tend to be on time or late, by custom?
- Weekday evenings are the most common times for official entertaining, leaving weekends and evenings for families.
- Review plans in terms of local food and drink preferences and entertaining space.
- How will the weather impact the event?
- What are the language abilities of proposed guests?
- Make a guest list that allows for both entertainment and policy advancement.
- Each member of the NGO should have target guests with whom to discuss issues.
- Invite diplomats and policy makers who might not share your opinions, not just the convinced.
- When sending an invitation to a formal event and/or official function, use official

stationery cards, followed by a telephone call. It is also acceptable to extend an invitation by telephone and to send a reminder card as a reminder, but sending the card in advance gives guests who might not immediately be prone to attend an NGO event a chance to read why they should attend, perhaps to meet a national figure in the movement.

- Make arrangements well in advance if equipment is to be borrowed or extra helpers hired. Include security and parking arrangements here, if appropriate. During a Presidential campaign I hosted an event in my house and used volunteers to organize local parking so that it would not disrupt the neighbors. After all, I had to live among them.

- For formal affairs, consider appropriate seating arrangements by taking into account the order of precedence of individuals in attendance. If confused, consult a professional protocol firm.

- Design seating arrangements after people arrive, not in advance, since some people would not respond, but attend anyway or accept but not attend. Invited guests will sometimes bring uninvited guests or arrive late. When it is crucial to have an accurate guest list, telephone the invitees to ask if they will attend.

- Name tags can be very useful for large informal events.

- Place cards are often used for formal dinners. When doing so, follow the rules of precedence. The male guest of honor sits to the right of the hostess and the female guests of honor to the right of the host. If there is no plan, invite the most important guests to the host's table. These are done in order by social ranking.

The following is one particular ranking order but ranking varies by country; to be safest, obtain a local protocol manual or call the Office of Protocol at the embassy of the country you will visit. (Leki, 2007)

1. Ambassador Extraordinary and Plenipotentiary
2. Ministers Plenipotentiary
3. Ministers
4. Chargé d'Affaires ad hoc or pro tempore
5. Charge d' Affaires ad interim
6. Minister-Counselors
7. Counselors (or Senior Secretaries in the absence of Counselors)
8. Army, Naval and Air Attachés
9. Civilian Attaches not in the Foreign Service
10. First Secretaries
11. Second Secretaries
12. Assistant Army, Naval and Air Attachés
13. Civilian Assistant Attaches not in the Foreign Service
14. Third Secretaries and Assistant Attachés

- Informal parties could be family-style meals, buffet lunches, barbecues, picnics, and teas.

- Even though informal entertaining is relaxed, keep in mind that the NGO staff is working. A backyard event involving hamburgers and cold drinks requires as much thought as a white tie State dinner. This is something any spouse of a diplomat will say.
- Make a List of People You and Your Staff Should Meet Either at a Personal Event or an Official Reception, making of whether the official has a topical responsibility, e.g., sustainable development, human rights perhaps the Security Council? Time is limited at a reception. Give priority to those covering critical issues.
- Place cards are used for formal dinners. When doing so, follow the rules of precedence. The male guest of honor sits to the right of the hostess and the female guests of honor to the right of the host. If there is no plan, invite ranking guests to the host's table.

Giving NGO's an Edge.

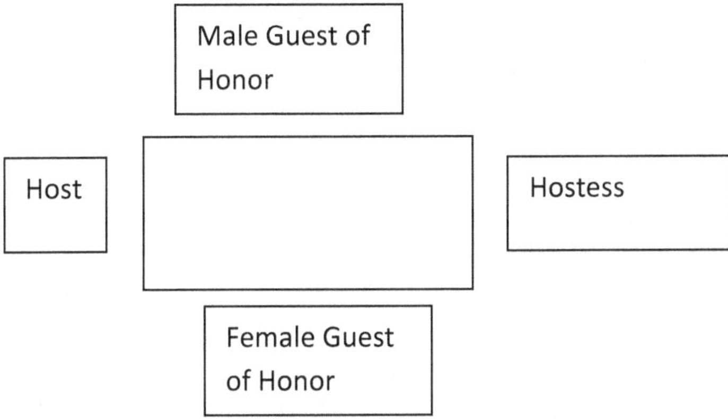

- Informal parties could be family-style meals, buffet lunches, barbecues, picnics and teas
- Even though informal entertaining is relaxed, keep in mind that the NGO staff is working. A backyard event involving hamburgers and cold drinks requires as much thought as a white-tie State dinner. This is something any spouse of a diplomat will say.
- Make sure to invite staff and friends from the NGO community and move the guests around so they can talk to different people, have a good time, while sharing ideas.
- A buffet service is an excellent format for breaking down formalities.
- Some guests do not like to eat from lap plates, so tables are a good idea, but keep them to no less than six, in order to stimulate conversation.

Use of Alcohol

Many NGOs have rules against paying for alcoholic drinks, and some do not allow them at all at a function, even if the staff members pay. While that is an internal matter for any NGO, be aware that alcohol is often served during diplomatic functions at the UN, the International Red Cross and Red Crescent Movement, the EC, and the World Bank. The main exception is an event in an Islamic culture. However, no one is going to force a delegate to drink or think less of the official for not drinking, except perhaps in in Russia or Japan where delegates are expected to drink, or at least take the alcohol that is offered. Pretend to drink. Depending on the circumstances, it is usually best to quietly avoid alcohol at social events, perhaps only sip a glass of wine or a highball glass of mineral water and lime, the theory being an official event is work, not vacation, and the head must be kept clear. That method has much precedent (House, 1926) and is increasingly normal. The real rule is never to overindulge at an event. If someone does get drunk on delegations, they should be sent back. Many CEO's do not care what employees do in their spare time; *never* do what the US Secret Service did in Cartagena in 2012.

Food at Social Events

Few issues are more controversial than food. Some people are vegans, vegetarians, or omnivores and some meat eaters won't eat particular kinds of animals; regardless of any internal food policy, NGOs wishing to work with International Organizations must be sensitive to local culture and understand that all IOs are a mix of omnivores, vegetarians, and vegans. This does not mean organizational standards need to be breached, but if a particular dietary style is to be offered at an NGO event, it is good idea to say so on the invitation card, and it may even be a good idea to provide a response card that allows the guests to note their requirements. Local cultural norms

should also not be violated, e.g., providing pork or alcohol in a Muslim gathering, pork at a Jewish gathering or beef at a Hindu party. On the other hand, when attending another's event, a delegate should accept offered food, unless he or she has some dietary restriction' then let the host know in advance. If a delegate cannot try a portion, just refuse with a simple explanation. However, if diet isn't a problem, consider new foods as an opportunity to explore a new culture and show it respect. Just keep in mind that in some cultures all of the served food should be eaten while in others a small portion is left on the plate.

Flags and Uniforms

Many NGO officials are former military or government officials, perhaps former officials at International Organizations, and may have been awarded official decorations that can be worn on civilian clothing. Doing so can be advantageous at a diplomatic function, though by wearing decorations, one might be conveying a partisan political point of view; so caution is advised. A precursor to the United Nations called the League of Nations, discouraged its officials during time of appointment from accepting honors from their government or decorations received prior to joining (Joyce, 1978, p. 77). The image was to be a servant of all humanity, not one nation.

Should the decision be to wear decorations, some experts suggest only doing it when the invitation says White Tie or Black Tie, "with decorations," and then of course wear them in correct order (French, 2010); decorations have always been in welcome at either Black Tie or White Tie events. It isn't required that the invitation allow it but keep in mind that most decorations are issued in two forms, one for day uniforms and one for tuxedos. Wear the smaller tuxedo variety in the correct order and make sure the delegate was awarded the decoration. In the United States, wearing unauthorized decorations can be a criminal offense under the Stolen Valor Act of 2005. In addition to legal issues, the taking on of unauthorized titles or wearing unearned medals is considered a serious breach of protocol. Every country has its own rules, so an NGO delegate wearing ribbons should wear them in the order of his or her own citizenship.

White-tie events are the most formal of evening dress events in Western society, whereas a black-tie event is

Figure 2 Private Collection, Larry Roeder

a normal evening affair. White House events are known to have both, and full State dinners are often white tie since the host and guests of honor are either heads of government or heads of state. Most formal events from inaugural balls to weddings to special receptions are usually black tie. For men the jacket can be either black or white.

An NGO wishing to hold a reception or meeting for many missions may find it useful to display national or organizational flags on a wall or walking path. Keep in mind customary rules when doing this and that flags change. One approach is to consult with the UN in New York which has a flyer on the order of flags. (Protocol and Liaison Service, United Nations, 2010).

When displaying flags, be certain to be accurate. Consider a formal briefing and reception I attended for the Foreign Minister of Somaliland at a hotel in Virginia, not long before I headed to his country to meet the President. The event had not started quite yet when the Minister noticed something odd about the national flag. It turned out the hotel staff had accidently turned it upside down, which is the international sign for distress. This kind of error is common, especially for horizontal tricolor flags; to prevent such a breach of etiquette, the NGO should obtain a manual of flags. Generally, the convention is that a national flag is only displayed on a car when the passenger is an Ambassador; that's not always so. One caution is worth mentioning. A flag is a national symbol; bearing it can convey the wrong message, and call into question an NGO's neutrality – especially since an NGO is never a national representative.

Other Issues at Receptions

- Events held in a UN compound are often possible, but if after hours, there will be an extra security fee. All guests will be required to have a grounds pass.
- **When inviting VIPs, "staff the invitation,"** meaning call the Mission or office and make sure that the assistant of whoever was invited receives a hard copy. If the NGO doing invitations has volunteers, do not mail any invitations; hands deliver them a month to 6 weeks in advance. That is a lot of work, but if the guest is important enough, he or she is important enough to verify receipt of the invitation.
- **Event Address**: Make sure the invitation has the right address, time and date. Human errors happen. One of the experts interviewed for this book remembered suggesting to an NGO that they hold their reception in a hotel across from UN HQ and volunteered to make arrangements, but the HQ wanted to do it because it handled the budget. Unfortunately, HQ staff (not familiar with New York) used the address of another hotel with the same name on the west side of Manhattan. The UN is on the east side, so the invitations had to be redone. Human errors will creep into even the most organized event; so it is best to have a local person manage such matters, and if possible have on the delegation one officer with that responsibility.
- **Mission Address**: Publications exist in every capital, in New York and Geneva showing

who represents what Mission or Embassy and their address and contact information, but these items often change without any warning. (Ad Hoc Working Group on Informatics, 2010).

- **Reserving Rooms**: Reserve a room for meetings or receptions six months in advance; national delegations and NGOs are doing the same. However, be aware that if the Secretary General or a national delegation wants the room, they will prevail, so have a fall back off-site venue.
- **Catering need not be problematic**. UNHQ in New York, UN agencies around the world, the International Red Cross and Red Crescent Movement, the EC and the World Bank in Washington all have contracted catering services, called concessions. NGOs should definitely host receptions because it is a great way to build exposure, but remember to work with the concession, which may require using their food and cost structure - for reasons of security. Concessions are however used to international audiences and should be able to handle any diet.
- **Have a backup plan**: Arrangements should be made prior to departure by the delegation, keeping in mind the budget, since catering can be very expensive. Determine if rooms are available at the conference site or hotel, nearby restaurants, and in the case of the conference site if the conference caterer must be used.

8 Ambassadors

Getting to know Ambassadors is essential. Ambassadors to the UN can help move initiatives along; so too Ambassadors to a nation's capital. For example, if an NGO wants the host government to agree to an international standard at the UN, while lobbying or negotiations will take place in New York or some other UN venue, if a friendly government shares the opinion of the NGO, then it also makes sense to approach that nation's representatives to the target country, ask their advice on tactics, who to approach in the local Ministries, etc. even to ask the Ambassador to speak on the issue's behalf. So, what is an Ambassador exactly, and is it ever appropriate for an NGO representative to take on such a title?

In the American system, the President decides who is an Ambassador, and this person must be confirmed by the Senate. The title is good for life. In UN agencies, goodwill Ambassadors are also created, but they only use the specialized title while serving in that capacity. In the British system, the UK Government uses the title Ambassador for the person formally accredited, through agreement by Her Majesty The Queen and the receiving government, as a head of a diplomatic mission in a non-Commonwealth country, whereas in British Commonwealth member countries, the head of diplomatic mission is known as a High Commissioner. There are a few exceptions, one of them being the Permanent Representative to the UN in New York, who is also called Ambassador. There will be other systems as well; international custom and law connotes special meaning to the term Ambassador, thus it is considered inappropriate for an NGO official to use the title unless they have been authorized by a government or an IO. Exceptions are found in a number of European countries which use the title in an honorific fashion and in some countries that permit individuals to retain the title of Ambassador once their tenure has finished (Morrin, 2010); great caution is recommended. When researching precedent for this book, there was discovered one official in a small European NGO who took on the title of Ambassador without ever having been granted the privilege by any IO or government. No protocol insult was intended; indeed, the otherwise inoffensive official just wanted to convey the diplomatic nature of her job; several proper Ambassadors did however comment that her approach was "uninformed." Why? An Ambassador symbolizes his or her country's sovereignty and is the personal representative of the head of government/state or IO (Leki, 2007).

Keep in mind that irrespective of the personal relationship an NGO representative might have with an Ambassador, everything said to this person is likely to be reported back to the Foreign Office/Ministry/Department of State. There are no off-the-record conversations. Ambassadorial duties include negotiating agreements (though often only with authority from the capital), reporting on political, economic and social conditions, advising on policy options, protecting national interests, and coordinating the activities of government agencies and personnel in the country. The point on authority is particularly pertinent to an NGO because if an Ambassador or some other official does not have instructions to support an NGO's cause, they might not have the liberty to be of help, no matter what they might say at a social event. In those situations, the best advice is to (a) ask to keep them up to date/brief on an informal basis and (b) lobby the Foreign Ministry in capital to provide instructions. Remember that regardless of the topic, without instructions from the Foreign Ministry, officials at an Embassy or Mission cannot do much.

Instead of using first names, always use the courtesy title, unless otherwise invited. Ambassadors are addressed as Mr. or Madam Ambassador, Ambassador Jones, Sir or Ma'am. Some countries do allow an Ambassador to keep his or her title after retirement, but this is not always the case and so NGO officials who used to be Ambassadors should avoid using the title unless they are certain the practice is authorized. Officials below Ambassador are called Mr., Ms., or Mrs., if marital status is known. Military officials go by rank, unless retired, then are called Mr. or Mrs., except for field and general grade officers, who generally are allowed to retain their titles (Leki, 2007).   The following is the American order of precedence: Ambassador Extraordinary, Charge d'Affaires;   Minister-Counselors; Counselors   (or Senior Secretaries in the absence of Counselors); Army, Naval, Civilian Attaches not in the diplomatic corps; First Secretaries; Civilian Assistants. (see also demarches) (Leki, 2007)

When a country has more than one Ambassador posted to multiple missions, the order of precedence among them is determined by the customs of their country. Keep in Mind that officials not in the formal diplomatic corps are also diplomats if they hold a diplomatic letter or a diplomatic passport and are on assignment.

9 Invitations and Greetings

As the diplomatic community gets to know an NGO officer, invitation to receptions will follow. Cultural differences abound in issuing and responding to invitations, so it is often best to consult with local authorities in advance. As a general rule, unless the invitation is addressed to other family members, they are not invited, including the spouse. Do not bring someone you are dating to a working event, unless allowed. Do respond by phone within two days. If the card says "regrets only," no response is needed unless you cannot attend. In that case, it is important to regret. If the card says "rsvp," always respond.

A few common greetings go a long way, as well as some food vocabulary in the host language in order to get through informal social situations. Be aware that cultures can vary dramatically in how they greet people. In Albania, people nod for no and shake their head for yes. Bows, handshakes and kisses, and other forms of friendliness can be decidedly different. In the Arab world, it is not uncommon to see men showing affection by holding hands while walking. The appropriate distance between people can be quite different than in the West. In China, people stand close in order to show trust. The best advice is to ask about such customs in advance, so not to be surprised. When confused, just ask during an event. Hosts are always willing to respond to a guest who expresses honest interest in their culture.

Introductions are an important part of an event, to exchange names. Keep it simple "Mrs. Clinton, may I present Mr. Lewis" is used in formal settings. In an informal setting, try Mrs. Clinton, Mr. Lewis." Do introduce yourself but just use your first and last name, never an honorific. It is also important for a delegate to add context that he or she is representing a particular kind of NGO. "Hello, I'm Dana Seagrams, Director for Disaster Management in the Society for the Protection of Cultural Centers in the in Gambia." Every culture has a way of asking how someone is and responding. Learn them, and keep in mind gender. When asking a male how do you do in Hebrew, it is Ma shlomkha? To a female it is Ma shlomekh? Smiles and a casual hello can be appropriate in cocktail parties. When introducing several people, start with the person of the highest rank and women. Any NGO attending diplomatic functions should also have a set of stories that link humor and the NGOs core mission, stories that seem naturally told and are memorable (unless meeting the same people often!).

- When making introductions, tell each individual a bit of information about the other; this encourages conversation
- Rise when meeting anyone or being introduced
- Learn the rules of greeting and leave-taking. Failure to use them is considered a serious breach of protocol and extremely rude.
- Don't panic if you forget names. If that happens, just say something like "Good evening, I'm Jim Smith of Human Rights, International. We met last year at the Navajo Indian conference in Window Rock, Arizona on the protection of indigenous cultures. Great to see you again." This reminds the other of the first meeting, provides a context in which to respond, and likely the delegate will reintroduce

himself. When unsure, begin by assuming the other does not remember you either. Give them a clue. On the other hand, if the referenced earlier meeting was wrong, this is not a problem. The other delegate will simply correct the error and likely provide lots of information.

10 Dress

The dress at most international conferences is Western business attire, but local clothes are also frequently worn, especially by indigenous guests or when making a cultural statement; and in some climates local clothing is also more practical. To be effective and respected, know the right dress and customs at the event you will attend. When in doubt, call the local UN office, the Embassy, or the Ministry or Agency which issued the invitation. If nothing else, this action alone will do much to reduce stress. International Conference negotiations can run into 12-14h days, so wear comfortable shoes. There is often not enough time to change clothes for evening receptions, so consider how to dress during the day to make sure it is appropriate for the evening. When the hotel is a long way away, it is a good idea to bring toothpaste and brushes, mouthwash and cologne, any daily medicine. Freshening up in the middle of a difficult day can do much to rebuild spirits and energy.

Semiformal/informal:

May be worn for cocktail parties, dinners, some dances, the theater, the opera, and evening receptions.

- Male Attire: Dark suit, Tie or bow tie, Dark shoes. Dinner suit is acceptable.
- Female Attire: Short cocktail dress, gloves are optional and rare to see, High-heeled shoes or dressy flats.

Casual Dress:

In the some countries, jeans or sportswear is often seen, also at casual functions in some diplomatic Missions. However, if invited to a casual dress affair, be aware that not everyone means jeans and sneakers. Business attire is usually appropriate for an event specified as casual. But call ahead. Breakfast, lunch, daytime meetings, afternoon tea, and some receptions are generally considered casual, but the invitation should specify.

- **Male Attire**: Business suit (light or dark) or Sports jacket and pants, Tie or bow tie, Dress shoes or loafers (called slip-ons or slippers in other cultures).
- **Female Attire**: Business suit or daytime dress as well as pumps or flat shoes;
- **Head coverings** may be considered a requirement at some events. Wide-brim hats may also provide welcome and necessary protection from the sun.

11   Gender and Race

Gender roles can be very complex.   Certainly as a topic of NGO advocacy, the community needs to acknowledge female strength and achievement, and remind other of the importance of succeeding in the ongoing global struggle for gender equality empowerment.   When about to enter a country for a negotiation or when engaging a diplomat or Minister from another country, inquire in advance about gender customs.

Even regions in a country can vary, especially one with a wide diversity of ethnic and religious groups.   When entertaining, spouses may have unexpected social rules in receiving lines or the dining table. Some cultures require clothing which in the NGOs land is not appropriate. Do not complain; instead, go along with these traditions, unless they are demeaning, show respect for local culture and remember that the role of the Delegation is not to change host country customs, but to advance the NGOs goals. When going to Mosques for example, take your shoes off. Woman should not show bare legs there and must cover their heads.

In an Islamic society, men should not offer to shake the hand of a woman, regardless of location. In any Islamic society, a man should instead wait for the woman to extend her hand to be shaken, rather than offering his hand first, and shake her hand only if she has given that signal. Men and women are unlikely to meet in a mosque since she would be on the women's balcony or rear seating area and he in the front or main floor, but even outside the mosque this etiquette should be followed. If addressing mosque etiquette for women, you should make sure to say that any female entering a mosque should have something handy to cover her head (doesn't have to be a scarf, a jacket can be used); though non-Muslim (especially Western) women are not expected to follow this rule completely, and may enter the mosque without a head cover if otherwise modestly attired, many women would likely feel more comfortable by having some form of head covering as a mark of respect for the location

There are some exceptions. One expert consulted on this book noted that when dealing with some cultures, it is wise not to have a female as the lead of the team or delegation; even people of certain religions as lead can be a problem. If you are dealing with diplomats or officials used to working with diplomats, they will usually accommodate. Field operations are another matter. Never endanger staff just to make a moral point like this.

12 Speak Without Notes

In many situations, a formal written speech is the proper format for communications, especially when speaking on the record where an interpreter will assist; he will need the exact words. But what about impromptu speeches given at receptions and cocktail parties? Delegates are going to hear a lot of speeches, especially at conferences, but even at dinner and cocktail parties. Instead of reading PowerPoint presentations or pages of speech, skip the props, except perhaps for one slide, practice the presentation three or four times, and then tell the story. The truth is that at conferences many read speeches are heard

Giving NGO's an Edge.

and forgotten. The passionate, from-the-heart speech will be remembered if it is well told.

13 Use of Language

Official and Working Languages

Working languages are used in a conference room during negotiations, or in the field. They can vary widely, from Swahili to Arabic. Although multilateral negotiations, especially in UN agencies, are mostly done in English, with intersperse of other languages, it isn't always so[3]. It is recommended having in the Delegation at least one person who can speak and write in the main working language[4].

Official languages If the negotiation will result in a written agreement, the language chosen for the text is the official language. For practical reasons, since hundreds of languages exist, some international organizations also have a limited set of official languages for conversations. The Arab Red-Cross

---

[3] Multilateral negotiations in the UN system, the World Bank, and the IFRC are generally in English, though the UN's official languages are Arabic, Chinese, English, French, Russian, and Spanish. The working languages of the General Assembly are English, French, and Spanish (in the Security Council only English and French are working languages), which is why those are really the only two languages needed when meeting with delegations to the UN in Geneva and New York. But different organizations have different rules.

[4] When I represented a British NGO in Tunis for negotiations with the Arab League and the Association of Red Cross and Red Crescent Societies, the discussions were entirely in Arabic, with simultaneous English interpretation, but IFRC talks in Geneva were in English with French and Arabic interpretation.

and Red Crescent Societies use Arabic and English, whereas the there are five official languages at the UN. If someone speaks in one, translation is often offered in the rest, but in any other, though translation from a non-official to an official may be offered. Further, the text must be in one of the official languages.

The French regularly insist on using their own language, and it is useful to note that at one time, the official language of diplomacy was French; that changed forever when the negotiators at Versailles agreed to British and American demands that the official languages of the League of Nations and its related bodies be both French and English (Miller, 1928, pp. Vol I, pg 505). Truth is, change was on its way. As late as 1903, French was the official language of the Interparliamentary Union, a precursor to the League (Bartholdt, 1930, p. 214). However, choices of official language began to change by 1895 when a tribunal of arbitration was held in Paris to settle differences between Great Britain and the United States on the Bering Straits. To the surprise of the French arbitrators, the United States insisted on English, but President Harrison did agree that official languages could also be those of other participants (Cambon, 1931, p. 113).

The bottom line on Language:

Determine what languages will be used in any situation related to a project and be able to operate in those languages, have a translator or arrange for the host to offer translation. Also agree on the official language for any Outcomes Document and make sure that before agreeing to a text, a true expert in that language translates[5] it. This person should also understand the subtleties of your language. If the translator does not fully grasp either language or the required terminology, e.g., jargon specific to the NGOs field of work then serious mistakes can be made[6].

Facilitators are also often used on field trips for getting through customs, interactions at farms, etc. Their role is to understand customary approaches to rules, often to smooth the edges, but a caution is in order because facilitators quite innocently can also take over a situation and lead a delegation where it does not wish to go. They also might miss something considered by the delegation as an opportunity. Perhaps the delegation wants to photograph a stable,

---

[5] "Interpreters" work with the spoken word and "translators" work with the written word.

[6] In this context, one of the interesting things highlighted by one of the surveys used in this book for research was the variety of language used for by the NGOs we contacted. While 70% spoke English as a primary language, followed by Spanish, French, Arabic, and Portuguese, a lot of local languages were also primary. This illuminates several issues. For one thing, some of those NGOs will have trouble communicating in the UN or other international forums unless they have on staff someone who speaks a major UN language like English, which is sort of a lingua franca. But alternatively, they provide a rich tapestry of tongues that can be used to better understand the needs of local culture, yet another reason for fully integrating them into the discussion on international rules. Many of the lesser used language are actually very important global languages, e.g., Russian, Italian, Greek, Swedish, Dutch, and Norwegian. Other languages were: Navajo, Bahasa, Bosnian, Catalan, Estonian, Hindi, Marathi, and Telugu, and others..

but the facilitator might not understand unless briefed in advance. Ask lots of questions. Do not let them spend hours and hours talking to the driver or bodyguard. Some of that is needed to smooth local relations, but they will be more useful if they constantly interact with the delegation; ask questions, clarify needs, etc.

Jargon and Speed:

Even if English is a working language, not everyone will be native in English, certainly not jargon and colloquialism. Speak at a speed that is easy to follow.

Simultaneous Texts:

Any final document should have agreed official language(s) and that whatever is agreed should receive a good linguistic scrub. That will be especially important should you encourage governments to implement an agreed text. You do not want there to be confusion over intent. Even NGO delegates who are expert in both official languages should keep both texts in front of them. It can be very helpful and create goodwill. It will also help sort through disagreements that arise from poor translation.

What if you Don't speak any of the Official or Working Languages?

This can happen when a visiting dignitary shows up to make a speech, not actually negotiate. In these situations, a written statement is provided the interpreter. In fact, the common practice is share any speech with the interpreters, regardless of the base language. It makes interpretation easier.

Trying to Change Text

If you are dissatisfied with a proposed text during a negotiation, do not give up trying to change because you are an NGO. Governments do respect the point of view of NGOs, if they are well stated. Just make sure that interventions are seen as within a "spirit of consensus." That provides a positive spin. This is important because delegations that hold up negotiations without an excellent reason (from the perspective of the conference) can be "isolated; " but it is needed to slow things up a bit while gathering argumentation, just ask the proposing party to "explain their proposed change."

14 Neutrality

A guiding principle of humanitarian affairs is that "humanitarian assistance must be provided in accordance with the principles of humanity, neutrality and impartiality (UNGA, 1991)."   In the real world, diplomacy is often partial, aiming to not just mediate between opposing forces; to cause specific change; diplomats, and especially NGO diplomats need to be humane, meaning polite, even to representatives advancing offensive policy positions. For the most part, it is also best to be neutral in political fights – unless that is the point of the intervention.   To be neutral, just be sensitive that language proposed by the NGO does not appear to be negative toward a particular country. For example, members of the Arab Group and the Organization of the Islamic Conference (OIC) regularly make efforts in New York and in conferences to insert language in resolutions and documents that explicitly or implicitly single out Israel for criticism. Unless the NGOs mission is to criticize a policy like the slaughter of civilians in Syria, regardless of one's point of view, stay out of such a difficult situation. Such arguments are often distractions from a core mission like protecting women and children, though that can at times seem counter-intuitive.   This however does not mean being silent about abuses. MSF is famous for being neutral, not taking sides; they speak loudly in order to reduce abuse.   "MSF's actions are guided by medical ethics and the principles of neutrality and impartiality; reserves the right to speak out to bring attention to neglected crises, to challenge inadequacies or abuse of the aid system, and to advocate for improved medical treatments and protocols." (MSF, 2011)[7] Yet, as already mentioned, MSF was the lead NGO asking for US military support in 2014 during the Ebola crisis in West Africa.

When thinking of knowing the other side, also keep in mind religion, especially when the negotiation is done in the field. What is the religion of the people with whom you will negotiate an issue, and how will they perceive you if of a different belief system? Humanitarian relief work isn't about advancing a

---

[7] MSF reserves the right to speak out to bring attention to neglected crises, to challenge inadequacies or abuse of the aid system, and to advocate for improved medical treatments and protocols. MSF medical teams often witness violence, atrocities, and neglect in the course of their work, largely in regions that receive scant international attention. At times, MSF may speak out publicly in an effort to bring a forgotten crisis to public attention, to alert the public to abuses occurring beyond the headlines, to criticize the inadequacies of the aid system, or to challenge the diversion of humanitarian aid for political interests.

religion. It is about reducing misery or building up an economy. Yet, even if an NGO intends to do the right thing, nothing can be more harmful that being insensitive. Witness the riots in Kabul in 2012 after US military forces accidently destroyed Korans. Or go back to the relief operations in Sudan, a country split between Muslim, Christians and Animists. Too often religious NGOs proselytize, which is totally inappropriate in emergency settings.   It is best to leave such things to the indigenous population, such as in Uganda where Catholics became Muslims during the Amin rule, and before then in order to go to a Catholic school, one had to be baptized. Even statistics on how many people are or not Christian is a political weapon. In other words, neutrality isn't just about politics. It is also about faith.

Neutrality vs. Sovereignty

Being neutral has its limits. One of the great things about NGOs like MSN is that they will speak up when they see a real abuse; that brings risk. Government diplomats are banned from interference in the internal affairs of host nations by the Convention on Diplomatic Relations, (Denza, 2008); though they can certainly lobby government officials for changes, sometimes at the behest of their Foreign Affairs Ministries, spurred on by the public back home, themselves driven by Public Diplomacy advanced by NGOs.   Indeed, the UN is not supposed to interfere in the internal affairs of nations, though the exception is when the State violates international norms, for example committing crimes against humanity[8]. Diplomats do speak with political dissidents, though in private; but if he or she tries to impact elections or assist a dissident group, that's considered interference in internal affairs; though often the acts are justified, it can result in a Diplomat being declared persona non-grata, since they can't be arrested. This is a reflection of the legal concept of the right to protect national sovereignty. If an NGO, particularly a foreign NGO, tries to do the same, they do not have diplomatic immunity and the staff can be arrested. I'm not arguing against interference, particularly in order to save lives; the context of this book is to advance diplomacy. How will being arrested advance diplomacy? It is a serious question an NGO needs to ask before engaging in this kind of direct action.

Lest NGOs think that a government's push back on NGO interference damages democracy, while in the real world, that's often certainly true, the very concept derives from historical actions to protect democracy. It all started with the French revolution, which created the Constitution of 1793 *Acte constitutionnel du 24 juin 1793*; that the French people do not interfere in the affairs of other states; the people (very important here, distinguishing between the people and the state) do not tolerate interference by other nations in their affairs. This document, which grew out of the Declaration of the Rights of Man and of the Citizen of 1789, essentially provided for the superiority of public sovereignty over national sovereignty; interference by foreign powers was seen as an attack on the people as a whole. Again, in defense of freedom against

---

[8] This was a serious issue at the start of the League of Nations discussions, with the Swiss insisting that the League have no authority over internal affairs **Invalid source specified.**.

totalitarianism, interference by NGOs can be a good thing; however, it can also be risky to the physical safety of NGOs in-country and can undermine diplomatic initiatives; take those issues into account.

15 Titles and Saying Hello and Goodnight

Forms of address for foreign government officials and people holding professional, ecclesiastical, or traditional titles vary among countries.   To be current, check with the local embassy or UN office. Here are some recommendations on typical title.

Diplomatic Titles

Chiefs of Mission: In general Mr./ Madam Ambassador works fine.   This also applies to an Ambassador with a military title.   Some diplomatic missions are led by Ministers, in which case the form is Mr./Madam Last Name.

Government Titles

This can vary widely by country, so it is best to consult directly with the UN mission of Embassy of the country in question.   In most cases, the spouse of a government official does not share the official's title with his/her spouse (i.e., the President's spouse is Mr./Mrs. Reagan or Ms. Lincoln).

Executive Branch

- Mr./Madam President

Giving NGO's an Edge.

- Mr./Madame Vice President
- Cabinet members are addressed as Mr./Madam Secretary except Mr./Madam Attorney General (Parliamentary systems use Ministers for Cabinet officers, but Federal systems like that of the United States of America do NOT have Ministers; instead they have Secretaries, which are different in rank to Secretaries in the UK system.
- Below the rank of Secretary, Government officials are addressed by their own name: Mr/Madam Reynolds, not Mr/Madam Undersecretary. Sometimes Undersecretaries, Assistant Secretaries, and Deputy Assistant Secretaries are addressed as Mr. or Madam Secretary, but it is best just say Mr., Ms., or Mrs. as appropriate.

Judicial Branch

- Mr./Madam Chief Justice
- Mr./Madam Justice.   Keep in mind that below the Chief Justice of the Supreme Court, justices are Associate Justices, whereas Appellate Judges are not Justices, only judges. When in doubt, call the court HQ.   Why does this matter? While most NGOs do not talk to the Judicial Branch, they probably should do, as those contacts can be very helpful towards understanding local legal customs.

Legislative Branch

In some parliamentary systems, the legislative and executive branches are combined, so it is possible to have a Prime Minister, who is addressed as Mr. or Mrs. Smith, Prime Minister of X

- Senate - Senator Collins, not Mr. Collins.
- House - Mr./Madam Speaker of the House, and Mr./Madam Rogers for a state representative. The titles "Congressman" and "Congresswoman" are becoming more common in social usage, but are not, strictly speaking, correct forms of address.

State and Provincial Government Titles

- Governor Collins
- Mayor Millville or Mr./Madam Millville

16   Letter Formats

The Démarche

A démarche is usually a written communication between governments or with an International Organization used to convey a complaint, make an alert or to state a position. NGOs don't do démarches by name; they often do the same thing in the form of a letter or memorandum, so it makes sense to use formats the diplomatic community is used to receiving. The first rule is to use precise text, include any necessary phrases of courtesy for first-person notes or letters; the text should be self-explanatory, understandable and independent of any other document or earlier correspondence.

- Do not use foreign words.
- Avoid abbreviations and little-known acronyms.
- Keep in mind that memoranda are not letters:

too often, the forms are mixed, which is unprofessional. Make letters look like letters, not memos and vice versa. A common mistake is to insert a subject line on the top of a letter. This is an error because the opening paragraph explains the topic in a letter; a subject line is superfluous.

- Get the main point across in the opening paragraph. Ambassadors and government leaders receive thousands of letters a year. They might not read past the first paragraph, so instead of using the opening paragraph to advertise your NGO, just state your request.
- Keep the main body of a letter to one and half pages or less, including the signature block, if possible. If a lot of background material must be shared, create one-page TABs such as are used in Decision Memoranda. This is because the person written to will be busy. Ambassadors would not read more than a page in the main memo, unless the issue is important to them, so this sense of importance also needs to be present.
- Never use window envelopes when writing to diplomats or government leaders. That is tacky and commercial, and can result in the envelope being tossed out.
- Some NGOs make it a habit to put their logo on each page, probably thinking it is a great way to advertise. This is tacky.

How to Address Letters

There are a number of formats that can be used in mailing letters, some more formal and elegant than others. The following format is recommended for the middle of the envelope, which should be orientated lengthwise.

<u>Sample When Writing to Ambassadors to the UN to be included</u>

Capacity: Always address the person in the capacity for which he or she is written. For example, if Ambassador Doe was the Ambassador of Spain to the UN and ECOSOC, but the letter is about ECOSOC,

His Excellency
(Dr.)(General)   John   Doe
Representative of Spain on the Economic and Social Council of the United Nations
Street Address
New York, New York 00017, USA

Many Ambassadors also represent their country in the Group of 77 at the United Nations, a very important block. If writing to an Ambassador in that capacity

His Excellency
(Dr.)(General) John Macintyre
Representative of Whatever to
The Group of 77 at the United Nations
United Nations Headquarters, Room S-3953 New York, New York10017, USA

Giving NGO's an Edge.

Salutation for Ambassadors

"Dear Ambassador Doe" is sometimes used, but the best salutation for an Ambassador is either Excellency or Dear Mr. (Mrs.) Ambassador. When writing to someone of lower rank, usually start with Sir/Madam: of course in situations where the person writing knows the person being written to, less formal approaches are often used.

Complimentary Close for Ambassadors

Yours Sincerely is fine, but ordinarily it is one of the following: Just use the word "sincerely" or

- Head of Mission, the last line is usually: Accept, Excellency, the (renewed - if the Head was written to before) assurances of my highest consideration. Note: Highest is used because the Ambassador is the personal representative of the head of state.
- Deputy Head of perhaps a Charge´ d'Affaires ad interim, the last line is usually: Accept Sir/Madam, the (renewed - if written to before) assurance of my high consideration.

Other Personalities

Position: The Speaker of the House

The Honorable Nancy
Pelosi
     Speaker of the House of
Representatives
          Washington, DC 20515

Giving NGO's an Edge.

Salutation: Dear Madam Speaker
Complimentary Close: Respectfully or Sincerely

Position: United States Representative

The Honorable James Doe
    Street address   (sometimes not in Washington)
City, including zip code

Salutation:
Dear Mr., Ms.,
or Mrs. Doe
Complimentar
y Close:
Sincerely

Position: United States Senator

The Honorable Nancy Harriman Fidelity
    United States Senate
        Washington, DC 20510

Salutation: Dear
Senator Fidelity
Complimentary Close: Sincerely

Position: Cabinet Member (Minister or Secretary)

The Honorable Hillary Clinton
    Secretary of State

of the United States
of America
        Washington,
DC 20520

Salutation: Dear Madam Secretary or
Dear Minister, depending on title
Complimentary Close: Respectfully or
Sincerely.

Memo Enclosures and Attachments

If there is only one, do not number it If only
one, say "Enclosure," not "Enclosures." Little
details like that matter. This is where flyers
are placed or long background paragraphs,
perhaps a backgrounder on the NGO. Use
this formulation and place it at the bottom of
the page about two lines below the signature
line.

Enclosure:
Background on the protection of Horses in Snow.
Here is the formulation for more than on
enclosure. Enclosures:
(1) Background on the Protection of Horses in Snow.
(2) Background on Protection of Animals in Floods

Label the attachment (also called Tabs). For
example, Tab One: Background
on the Protection of Horses in Snow or
Background on the Protection of Horses
in Snow. Only number Attachments if there is

Giving NGO's an Edge.

more than one. Attachment One: Background
on the Protection of Horses in Snow.

Works Cited

Abshire, D. B. (2005). *The Character of George Marshal.*
     Lexington, Virginia: Washington and Lee University.

Ad Hoc Working Group on Informatics. (2010, June 13). *United
     Nations Members States.* Retrieved from Permanent
     Missions to the United Nations:
     http://www.un.int/index-en/index.html

Bartholdt, R. (1930). *From Steerage to Congress.* Philadelphia:
     Dorrance.

Boritz, M. (1998). The Hidden Culture of Diplomatic Practice.
     Ethnologia Scandinavica, pp. 48 - 62.

Boritz, M. (2010, September 21). Email Discussion on Diplomatic
     Practice. (L. Roeder, Interviewer)

Cambon, J. (1931). *The Diplomatist.* (C. R. Turner, Trans.) Philip
     Allan.

Denza, E. (2008). *Diplomatic Law, Commentary on the Vienna
     Convention on Diplomatic Relations.* Oxford: Oxford
     University Press.

French, M. M. (2010). *United States Protocol.* NY: Roman and
     Little Fittlefield.

Giving NGO's an Edge.

House, E. M. (1926). Conversation with the Chancellor of
        Germany. In C. Seymour, *Intimate Papers of Colonel
        House* (p. 142). New York: Houghton Mifflin.

Jordan, R. (2012, 8 8). Discussion on Security. (L. Roeder,
        Interviewer)

Joyce, J. A. (1978). *Broken Star.* Llandybie, Wales: Davies.

Lamont, T. W. (1921). Reparations. In E. M. House, & C.
        Seymour, *What Really Happened At Paris* (pp. 259-291).
        NY: Scribners.

Leki, R. (2007). *Protocol for the Modern Diplomat.* Washington,
        DC: Foreign Service Institute.

McCaffree, M. J., & Innis, P. B. (1977). *Protocol: The Complete
        Handbook of Diplomatic, Official and Social Usage.* NY:
        Prentice-Hall.

Miller, D. H. (1928). *The Drafting of the Covenant.* New York:
        Putnam.

Morrin, J. (2010, July 24). Interview by Email with Joanna
        Morrini, Ceremonial Office, Protocol Directorate,
        Foreign and Commonwealth Office. (L. Roeder,
        Interviewer)

MSF. (2011, December 1). *About MSF.* Retrieved March 8, 2012,
        from MSF: http://www.msf.org/

Protocol and Liaison Service, United Nations. (2010). *The United
        Nations Flag Code- ST/SGB/132 .* Retrieved from
        Protocol and Liaison Service:
        http://www.un.int/protocol/communication.html

Giving NGO's an Edge.

Roeder, L. W., & Simard, A. (2013). *Diplomacy and Negotiation for Humanitarian NGOs* . NY: Springer Science+Business Media.

UN. (2005, May 29). *News and Media.* Retrieved July 2011, from United Nations: http://www.unmultimedia.org/photo/detail.jsp?id=769/76989&key=11&query=cattle&sf=

UNGA. (1991, Dec 19). UNGA Resolution A/46/182. *Strengthening of the Coordination of Humanitarian Emergency Assistance of the UN*. New York: UN.